Strong Trucks

Written by Sarah Snashall

Collins

Strong trucks do all sorts of strong jobs.

digger

forklift truck

tipper

stunt truck

dumper truck

3

This stunt truck has deep grips
to stop skids.

They smash scrap cars and bump up ramps.

The hammer on this truck splits rocks from the cliff.

The biggest dumper trucks shift the biggest rocks.

The digger digs a trench.

Next, a tipper truck tips in the grit.

The long arm swings right into the house.

The forklift truck brings a stack of bricks.

At the scrapyard, magnets lift bits of cars.

The truck drops the scrap into the crusher.

Trucks

After reading

Letters and Sounds: Phase 4

Word count: 100

Focus on adjacent consonants with short vowel phonemes, e.g. *scrap*.

Common exception words: there, are, all, of, they, the, into, house, do, to

Curriculum links (EFYS): Expressive Arts and Design

Curriculum links (National Curriculum, Year 1): Design and Technology

Early learning goals: Reading: read and understand simple sentences; use phonic knowledge to decode regular words and read them aloud accurately; read some common irregular words; demonstrate understanding when talking with others about what they have read

National Curriculum learning objectives: Reading/word reading: read accurately by blending sounds in unfamiliar words containing GPCs that have been taught; Reading/comprehension: understand both the books they can already read accurately and fluently and those they listen to by checking that the text makes sense to them as they read, and correcting inaccurate reading

Developing fluency

- Encourage your child to follow the words as you read the first pages with expression.
- Take turns to read a page, encouraging your child to emphasise words that show each truck's strength.

Phonic practice

- Practise reading words that contain adjacent consonants. Encourage your child to sound out and blend the following:

  ramps   brings   cliff   swings   splits   trench

- Focus on double syllable words. Check your child includes all the sounds, for example check they do not miss "l" in **forklift**.

  bucket   forklift   dumper   magnets   scrapyard

Extending vocabulary

- Challenge your child to think of a word with a similar meaning to these verbs:

  smash (e.g. *destroy, squash*)   splits (e.g. *breaks, divides*)
  shift (e.g. *remove, take away, move*)   lift (e.g. *raise, carry*)